WOMEN IN THE CIVIL WAR

Essential Library

An Imprint of Abdo Publishing
abdopublishing.com

ESSENTIAL LIBRARY OF
★ THE CIVIL ★
WAR

BY KARI A. CORNELL

CONTENT CONSULTANT

BONNIE LAUGHLIN-SCHULTZ, PHD
ASSISTANT PROFESSOR OF HISTORY
EASTERN ILLINOIS UNIVERSITY

abdopublishing.com

Published by Abdo Publishing, a division of ABDO, PO Box 398166, Minneapolis, Minnesota 55439. Copyright © 2017 by Abdo Consulting Group, Inc. International copyrights reserved in all countries. No part of this book may be reproduced in any form without written permission from the publisher. Essential Library™ is a trademark and logo of ABDO Publishing.

Printed in the United States of America, North Mankato, Minnesota

052016
092016

THIS BOOK CONTAINS
RECYCLED MATERIALS

Cover Photo: Alexander Gardner/Buyenlarge/Getty Images
Interior Photos: Alexander Gardner/Buyenlarge/Getty Images, 1; North Wind Picture Archives, 4, 7, 14, 81, 86; Red Line Editorial, 9; Kean Collection/Archive Photos/Getty Images, 10, 34; Library of Congress, 17, 25, 26, 41, 42, 48, 56, 64, 69, 77, 84, 91, 99 (top), 99 (bottom); Buyenlarge/Getty Images, 18, 46; ClassicStock/Alamy, 23; Hulton Archive/iStockphoto, 31; Fotosearch/Getty Images, 36, 51; MPI/Getty Images, 45, 58; Hulton Archive/Getty Images, 60; J. W. Umpehent, 71, 98 (bottom); John Dainty, 72, 98 (top); Time Life Pictures/Timepix/The LIFE Picture Collection/Getty Images, 74; Lewis C. Lockwood/Project Gutenberg, 83; Tom Allen/The Washington Post/Getty Images, 93; Popperfoto/Getty Images, 95

Editor: Rebecca Rowell
Series Designers: Kelsey Oseid and Maggie Villaume

Cataloging-in-Publication Data

Names: Cornell, Kari A., author.
Title: Women in the Civil War / by Kari A. Cornell.
Description: Minneapolis, MN : Abdo Publishing, [2017] | Series: Essential library
    of the Civil War | Includes bibliographical references and index.
Identifiers: LCCN 2015960309 | ISBN 9781680782806 (lib. bdg.) |
    ISBN 9781680774696 (ebook)
Subjects: LCSH: United States--History--Civil War, 1861-1865--Women--
    Juvenile literature. | United States--History--Civil War, 1861-1865--
    Participation, Female--Juvenile literature.
Classification: DDC 973.7082--dc23
LC record available at http://lccn.loc.gov/2015960309

CONTENTS

A NATION DIVIDED

July 21, 1861, was no ordinary Sunday for Franklin Thompson, a 19-year-old private in the Union army's Second Michigan Infantry. Instead of church bells ringing out across the countryside, announcing the start of worship services, the sound of gunfire filled the air as soldiers from the North and the South fought near Manassas Junction, Virginia. The clash would become known as the First Battle of Bull Run.

That skirmish was the first major battle of the American Civil War (1861–1865). It was also the first time Thompson saw military action. All around, artillery boomed while steel swords clanged and muskets fired. Then, for the first time, Thompson saw a man die. An artillery shell exploded in a nearby battery, killing the gunner and injuring three other soldiers. Moments later, as the commanding colonel shouted orders to his men, a bullet zoomed past his head, nearly striking him. That bullet shot a hole in Thompson's flask. No place was safe. By the time the gunfire stopped, wounded, dying, or already dead soldiers covered nearly every inch of the field. Thompson described the scene: "The sight of that field is perfectly appalling. . . legs, arms, and bodies are crushed and broken as if smitten by thunder-bolts; the ground is crimson with blood; it is terrible to witness."[1]

For Thompson, that day at Bull Run would merge with many other brutal, gruesome days on the battlefield. But Thompson was no ordinary soldier. Franklin Thompson was actually Sarah Emma Edmonds. For Edmonds, dodging gunfire and witnessing the death of fellow soldiers would become commonplace. And she was not alone in her experience as a woman on the battlefield. Edmonds was one of a few hundred women who disguised their identities to fight with the Union or the Confederacy in the Civil War. She and other American women would serve in a variety of roles, including field nurse and spy, all of them doing what they could to support their side in a conflict that divided the United States and its citizens.

NORTH VERSUS SOUTH

The Civil War had been going on for three months when Edmonds experienced that unforgettable day at Bull Run. The war started before sunrise on

April 12, 1861. At 4:30 a.m. that day, a ten-inch (25 cm) mortar round exploded 100 feet (30 m) above Fort Sumter in South Carolina. With a loud blast, this bomb brought to life a conflict that had been brewing in American politics for many years.

The Confederate attack did not surprise the Union troops in command at the fort. On December 20, 1860, South Carolina had seceded from the Union, and the Union-held fort defended Charleston Harbor, a strategic port for the South. In January 1861, Mississippi, Florida, Alabama, Georgia, and Louisiana joined South Carolina in secession. These states formed their own nation, the Confederate States of America, in February. More

Residents of Charleston, South Carolina, watch the attack on Fort Sumter.

states would join over the next few months. Now, with the nation divided into North and South, an attack seemed imminent.

STATES SECEDE

Following Abraham Lincoln's election to the US presidency in November 1860, Southern states began to secede from the Union over the next several months:

- South Carolina, December 20, 1860
- Mississippi, January 9, 1861
- Florida, January 10, 1861
- Alabama, January 11, 1861
- Georgia, January 19, 1861
- Louisiana, January 26, 1861
- Texas, February 1, 1861
- Virginia, April 17, 1861
- Arkansas, May 6, 1861
- North Carolina, May 20, 1861
- Tennessee, June 8, 1861

After enduring 34 hours of continuous shelling, Union major Robert Anderson surrendered Fort Sumter to Confederate brigadier general P. G. T. Beauregard on April 13. In the hours that followed, Confederate supporters gathered in Charleston, South Carolina, to celebrate and cheer as boats in the harbor blared their horns in support.

News of the surrender shocked Northerners. Still, the mood in Northern cities was patriotic and upbeat. President Abraham Lincoln immediately called for 75,000 volunteer soldiers to join the fight against the Southern rebellion, and Northerners responded quickly.[2] In Boston, Massachusetts, journalist Mary Livermore witnessed support for the men who agreed to serve. She noted how "windows were flung up; and women leaned out into the rain, waving flags and

BRITISH NORTH AMERICA

New Hampshire
Vermont
Maine
Minnesota
Michigan
Wisconsin
New York
Massachusetts
Rhode Island
Connecticut
Oregon
Dakota Territory
Washington Territory
Iowa
Pennsylvania
New Jersey
Delaware
Maryland
Nevada Territory
Nebraska Territory
Utah Territory
Colorado Territory
Illinois
Ohio
Indiana
West Virginia
Virginia
Kansas
California
Missouri
Kentucky
North Carolina
New Mexico Territory
Indian Territory
Tennessee
South Carolina
Arkansas
Georgia
Pacific Ocean
Alabama
Atlantic Ocean
Texas
Mississippi
Louisiana
Florida
THE BAHAMAS
MEXICO
Gulf of Mexico

Union states without slavery
Union states and regions with slavery
Confederate states
Territories

South Carolina's secession in December 1860 divided the nation and led to ten more states seceding by the middle of 1861.

handkerchiefs" as volunteer soldiers made their way through the streets to report for duty.[3]

WOMEN STEP UP

As men marched off to war, women looked for ways they could contribute to the cause. Many women on both sides of the conflict began gathering food, clothing, bandages, and other supplies. They stockpiled such items in their homes, planning to send the goods to the troops as needed. Women also began organizing aid societies. These volunteer groups were dedicated to making much-needed items for soldiers. Southern groups included the Ladies' Relief Society of Lynchburg, Virginia, and the Ladies Association in Aid of the Volunteers of the Confederate Army of Greenville, South Carolina. Northern organizations included the Ladies Aid Society of Columbus, Ohio.

Sarah Emma Edmonds was one of at least a few hundred women who fought in the Civil War.

Thousands of women also volunteered as nurses. They were inspired by stories of Florence Nightingale, a British nurse famous for improving sanitary conditions and patient recovery rates in Europe and Asia during the Crimean War (1853–1856). These women left home to serve their militaries. Northern women traveled to Washington, DC, and to Southern battlefields to care for the ill and wounded. Southern women treated soldiers on the battlefield or in makeshift hospitals in churches or private homes.

A few women, such as Edmonds, went as far as disguising themselves as men and fighting on battlefields. Many fought bravely alongside male soldiers who valued their female comrades' contributions. These women soldiers often went undetected until they were injured or killed in battle.

ON THE HOME FRONT

With battles sometimes waged in their backyards, Southern women endured

SEPARATE SOCIAL SPHERES

The American Civil War erupted during the Victorian era (1837–1901). During this era, middle- and upper-class women and men functioned in different areas of society, an idea known as the doctrine of separate spheres. Men led public lives, leaving home each day to make money for the family. Women stayed home to care for the children, cook, and clean. These separate spheres made women subservient to men. Still, women discovered power in their socially defined sphere. They used it to gain independence as they formed aid societies, which performed charitable work that was considered part of their sphere. Women had little time for socializing. When they did socialize, women were expected to follow a strict code of conduct, including keeping their opinions to themselves. Also, women were not allowed to vote and could not own property.

hardships most Northern women did not. Soldiers from both sides stole food from gardens, killed livestock, and plundered firewood and other items. Southern women also lived through food shortages that sometimes led to rioting. On Southern plantations, wives took over managing all household duties, including overseeing the slaves who worked in the cotton fields, a task usually done by men. For female slaves and working-class white women in the South, the war meant they had to double their workload to cover the jobs of men who had gone to work or fight in the war.

While the lives of wealthy Northerners were relatively unaffected by the war, well-to-do women often participated in the war effort by organizing benefits and fund raisers. Meanwhile, working-class Northern women filled in for men who were away at war. Pay varied by job. Women earned more money working at mills and artillery manufacturing plants than at textile factories. All the jobs provided much-needed income. Many women also filled teaching positions that opened during and after the war. Women's aid societies, including some all-black groups, arranged for these new teachers to tutor former slaves in reading, writing, and life skills.

STEPPING OUT OF THE SHADOWS

The Civil War provided Northern and Southern women alike with countless opportunities to support their troops and manage their home fronts. Along the

THE AFTERMATH OF THE CIVIL WAR

Both the North and the South suffered tremendous losses during the war, but the South emerged with many more battle scars. Because the majority of the war was fought in Confederate states, much of the South had to be rebuilt, including Atlanta, Georgia, and Charleston, South Carolina. A particularly devastating loss was the South's transportation network. Union forces had targeted the railroad system, destroying bridges, tracks, and rail yards in an effort to stop the movement of Confederate troops. In the postwar era, the damaged transportation system kept the South from moving the food and goods it produced to market.

way, they gained skills in organizing relief efforts, managing households, and recruiting volunteers. Many also found their activist voices. These skills became the foundation upon which women continued to build the case for equal rights for all Americans, regardless of sex or color.

The American Civil War was instrumental in bringing many women out of the shadows of men, inspiring those women to consider their personal thoughts on slavery. Numerous women in the North and some in the South rallied behind the Emancipation Proclamation. They appreciated it in the context of their own lack of freedom as a group within American society. The war was costly in its destruction of lives and property. It also proved invaluable as a testing ground for women. Whether they were white or black, Northern or Southern, women showed themselves brave, proud, strong, smart, and far more capable than their society credited them.

ORGANIZING FOR CAUSES

In the years leading up to the Civil War, a growing number of Northern women became active in social causes aimed at moral reform. These included temperance, abolishing slavery, improving prison conditions, and women's rights. These calls for reform stemmed, in part, from a religious movement called the Second Great Awakening, which swept the nation in the early to mid-1800s. The Second Great Awakening stressed that people had free will and the ability to take action and change society for the better. Most important, the religious movement welcomed the participation of all women, no matter their skin color, and encouraged them to play a greater role in social reform.

WOMEN'S AID SOCIETIES

Soon after the first shots were fired at Fort Sumter in April 1861, women in the North and the South responded with zeal. They quickly formed aid societies to provide soldiers with both necessities and the comforts of home. These social groups met on a regular basis to make items for the troops. Members spent their spare moments knitting socks, mittens, and hats and sewing shirts and quilts to keep soldiers warm on the battlefield. Women also gathered food and medical supplies for troops and raised money for the war effort. These societies numbered approximately 7,000 in the Northern states and the West.[1] Volunteers also canned vegetables from their gardens or baked sweets to send to Union camps.

The first recorded women's aid society in the North formed in Bridgeport, Connecticut, on April 15, 1861, shortly after the attack at Fort Sumter. Its members knitted socks, made quilts, and sewed shirts for the soldiers. Similar organizations quickly followed, including the Ladies Hospital Aid Society, the Union Volunteer Refreshment Saloon, and the US Christian Commission. Most of these groups tended to be segregated by class. Societies established by white women consisted of members of the middle and upper classes. Working-class women usually had little time for such activities. These groups preferred to send the items they made and collected exclusively to soldiers from local regiments who were on the front lines.

In the South, shortages in warm clothes and shoes began to take their toll on Confederate soldiers by the winter of 1861–1862. The Northern blockade prevented wool, cloth, clothing, and other goods from reaching Southern states. In response to these shortages, Southern women formed their own women's aid societies. Confederate women joined more than 1,000 such groups, which sprouted up in Southern cities or were organized by existing church groups.[2] Groups such as the Ladies' Aid Association of Greenville, South Carolina, the Ladies' Relief Society in Lynchburg, Virginia, the Charleston Soldiers Relief Association,

Women used posters to advertise aid society fund-raising events.

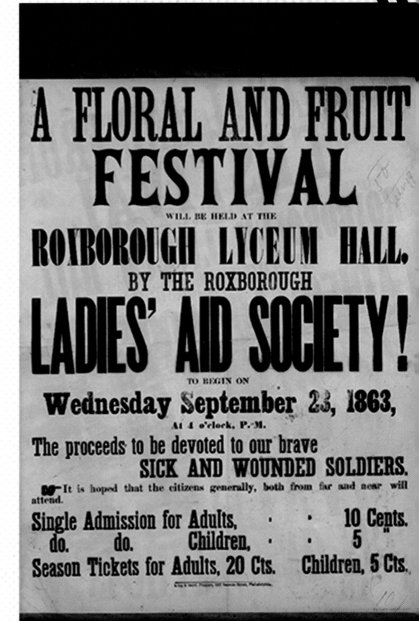

A FLORAL AND FRUIT FESTIVAL
WILL BE HELD AT THE
ROXBOROUGH LYCEUM HALL,
BY THE ROXBOROUGH
LADIES' AID SOCIETY!
TO BEGIN ON
Wednesday September 23, 1863,
At 4 o'clock, P. M.
The proceeds to be devoted to our brave SICK AND WOUNDED SOLDIERS.
It is hoped that the citizens generally, both from far and near will attend.
Single Admission for Adults, · · 10 Cents.
do. do. Children, · · 5
Season Tickets for Adults, 20 Cts. Children, 5 Cts.

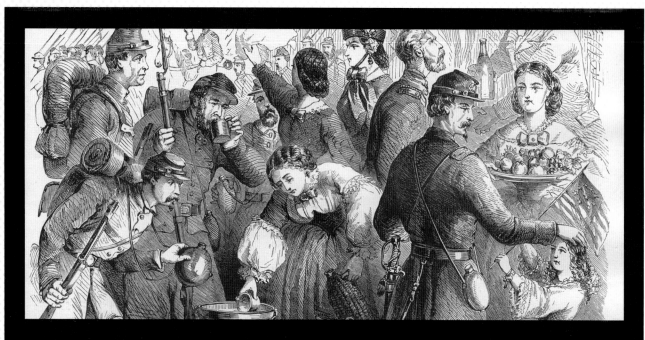

Women helped soldiers in a variety of ways, including by providing them with food and drink.

and the Mobile Military Aid Society in Alabama pooled their resources and did what they could to support Confederate troops. These groups organized clothing drives, urging Southern families to donate wool sweaters, coats, or pants to keep the soldiers warm. Women even resorted to cutting up rugs and stitching them together to make blankets for the soldiers.

Volunteers in the aid societies on both sides of the conflict also planned events or went door to door to raise money for the troops. In the North, the US Sanitary Commission promoted fund-raising fairs called sanitary fairs, which brought in considerable amounts of money. A fair held in Chicago, Illinois, in October 1863 brought in $100,000 for Union troops, and an April 1864 fair in New York City, New York, made approximately $2 million.[3] In the North, many middle- and upper-class women liked to attend the fairs because they provided a way to both support the war effort and socialize.

Aid societies sent troops handmade clothing and knits in what are now commonly referred to as care packages. They were also filled with favorite homemade jams and jellies, brandy and other spirits, books, and chicken soup to comfort loved ones who fell ill. But many supplies sent from the North and the South did not reach the intended recipients because they were intercepted or stolen along the way.

Volunteers in the North and in the South became discouraged that sweaters knit with love or favorite canned goods never reached loved ones on the front and stopped trying to send packages. In some instances, when army camps were not too far away, women took it upon themselves to deliver their own packages.

As the war dragged on, some Northern aid organizations disbanded due to frustration over packages not reaching their intended recipients. Groups in the South, however, faced a different dilemma. One year into the war, supplies and food dwindled in the South, making it difficult for Confederate aid organizations to continue sending supplies to the troops. Many of these organizations had no choice but to disband.

THE ABOLITIONIST MOVEMENT

Thirty years before the Civil War began, some women, mostly in the North, got involved in the abolitionist movement. They wrote articles for abolitionist newspapers such as the *Liberator*, handed out pamphlets declaring the evils of slavery, petitioned Congress to end slavery, and called for others to join them in the fight to end the practice. Some women offered their homes as stops on the Underground Railroad, a network of secret routes (called lines) and safe houses (called stations) that existed in 14 states, providing fugitive slaves with a path to freedom in the North. Others made speeches at abolitionist gatherings. Several abolitionist women, including sisters Sarah Moore Grimké and Angelina Grimké Weld, also fought for women's rights.

The November 1860 election of Abraham Lincoln, the first president with strong antislavery leanings, provided hope to some abolitionists, including Maria Patec of Manhattan, Kansas. She wrote to her cousin in New England of an impending war over the practice:

> *The time has come I think, when the battle of Armageddon is to be fought, the day of preparation is at hand, the irrepressible conflict has begun as in the days of the Israelites in Egypt. God will no sooner look [favorably] upon bondage in America than he did in Egypt.*[4]

Patec's words would prove true as the issue of slavery divided the nation. The war would provide opportunities for the enslaved to gain freedom and Northern women to offer aid to the newly freed.

HELP FOR FREED SLAVES

As the Civil War unfolded and Union troops began to take over territory in Southern states, many slaves ran for freedom across Union lines. The freed slaves arrived hungry and tired, wearing tattered clothing and desperate for a place to stay. Many of the new arrivals lived in makeshift refugee camps, where conditions were poor at best.

Organizations such as the Contraband Relief Association in Washington, DC, and the Chicago Colored Ladies' Freedmen's Aid Society, whose members were African American, formed to raise money and deliver food and clothing to people in the camps. Many women volunteered in the camps, nursing the ill and helping them get settled. Abolitionist women, both black and white, helped gather supplies for freed slaves, gave them a place to stay until they were able to support themselves, and worked to find jobs for the new arrivals.

AFRICAN-AMERICAN AID SOCIETIES

White women were not the only group to form aid societies. In the North, some black women joined African-American aid societies, which were called colored aid societies, reflecting the language of the time. Their members produced goods to send to soldiers and to freed slaves. Organizations such as the Colored Women's Sanitary Commission and the Ladies' Sanitary Association of Saint Thomas's African Episcopal Church formed in Philadelphia, Pennsylvania.

ABOLITION
THE BEGINNING OF A WOMEN'S MOVEMENT

In the years leading up to the Civil War, women got involved in the abolitionist movement by the thousands. They wrote articles for abolitionist newspapers, distributed pamphlets declaring the evils of slavery, petitioned Congress to end slavery, and called for others to join them in the fight to end the practice.

But when politically active women such as Lucretia Mott and Elizabeth Cady Stanton tried to attend the World Anti-Slavery Convention in London, England, in 1840, they were not allowed to participate because they were female. Abolitionist sisters Angelina Grimké Weld and Sarah Moore Grimké endured discrimination from men within the movement for their "unwomanly behavior," which consisted of speaking against slavery at abolitionist gatherings.[5] This exclusion from the abolitionist movement prompted several women, including Mott and Stanton, to band together to fight for women's rights.

As the Civil War began, however, many leaders within the two movements urged all women to set aside women's rights and focus on ending slavery. Working together, women from both movements pushed for the government to pass the Thirteenth Amendment, which abolished slavery, and the Fourteenth Amendment, which forbid discrimination on the basis of race. The experience of organizing to end slavery laid a strong foundation for the fight for women's rights that was yet to come.

Lucretia Mott, *center*, sometimes faced angry mobs because of her support for abolition.

> "I think it is our duty as a people to spend our lives in trying to elevate our own race. Who can feel for us if we do not feel for ourselves? And who can feel the sympathy that we can who are identified with them?"[8]
>
> —E. Garrison Jackson, a black woman from Rhode Island, in her application to teach in the South for the American Missionary Association

Many other women who were not necessarily active participants in the abolitionist movement traveled south during the war to teach former slaves to read and write. Women's aid societies, freemen's societies, the American Missionary Association, and religious organizations paid to send 900 teachers to Union-occupied areas of the South, such as Sea Islands, South Carolina.[6] Three-fourths of these teachers were women.[7] In addition to reading and writing, all teachers instructed their students on keeping house, paying bills, and finding jobs. Only a handful of occupations, including working in cotton fields, sewing, or housekeeping, were available to African-American women at the time.

Throughout the war years, women in the North and the South—white and black—lent a hand to those in need. Their handmade gloves, hats, and sweaters not only kept soldiers warm on the battlefield but also boosted morale by serving as a reminder of loved ones back home. In the same spirit, women abolitionists and aid society members helped ease the transition of former slaves into society. But some women yearned to do more. They wanted to take a more active role in the conflict itself.

Women sent by the American Missionary Association to teach former slaves in South Carolina pose for a photograph while two students nearby hide their faces.

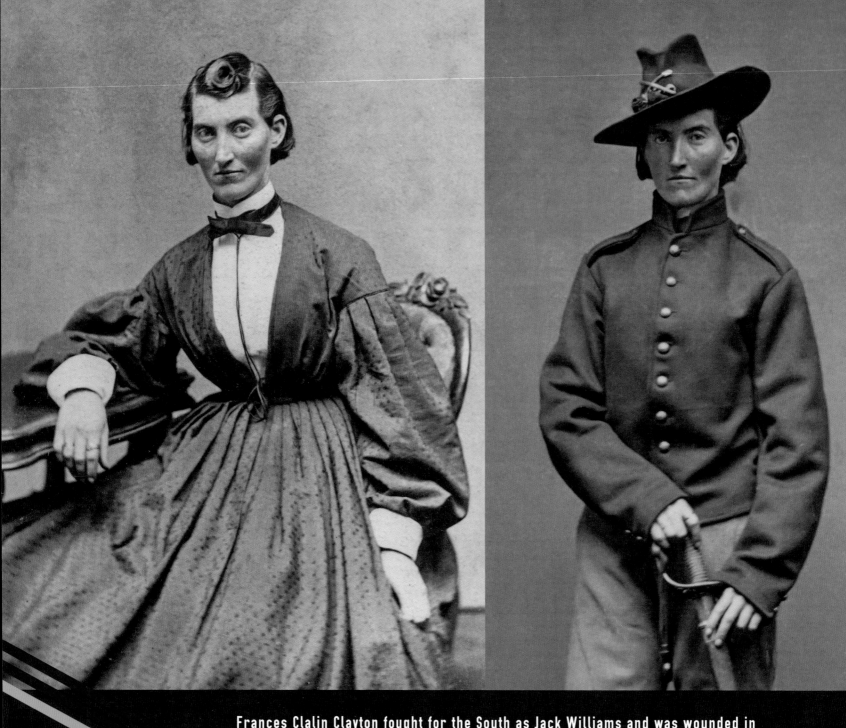

Frances Clalin Clayton fought for the South as Jack Williams and was wounded in the Battles of Shiloh and Stone River.

CHAPTER 3

FIGHTING AS SOLDIERS

When Sarah Emma Edmonds fought at the First Battle of Run on July 21, 1861, she was not the only woman on the battlefield. Five others fought as well. Louisa Hoffman fought for the Union as part of the First Ohio Infantry. A woman known simply as Charlie also took up arms on the Union side. So did Frances Jamieson, a first lieutenant from Kentucky who used the name Frank Abel and fought under her husband, who was a captain. On the Confederate side, Loreta Janeta Velazquez fought as a lieutenant using the name Harry T. Buford. In fact, women dressed as male soldiers fought in nearly every major Civil War battle.

Joining the army during the Civil War was not difficult for women. Because both sides were desperate for soldiers, doctors conducting medical exams typically checked only enlistees' teeth and made sure they could hold and fire a rifle properly. For many women, most of whom lived or had grown up on farms, firing a rifle was second nature.

Assuming the look of a soldier was also relatively easy. Civil War uniforms were loosely cut, which allowed women to hide breasts or hips and bulk up slender waists to look more masculine. And their lack of facial hair was not a problem. Recruiting offices needed soldiers, especially in the South, where there was no age restriction for joining a regiment. As a result, it was common for teenage boys and young men—many of whom lacked facial hair—to join the military. Still, some women, including Velazquez, disguised themselves further by wearing a false mustache or beard.

Once in the field, keeping their identities a secret was not too challenging. Regiments were always on the move, and soldiers slept in canvas tents or with a bedroll under the stars. There were no public toilets or bathhouses. Soldiers slept in their clothes, washed alone in a stream or river, and snuck off into the woods to relieve themselves. And many women stopped having their menstrual periods as a result of constant marching and not having enough food to eat.

UNKNOWN NUMBER OF WOMEN SOLDIERS

Historians have officially documented only 250 female soldiers.[1] However, some sources estimate the actual number is somewhere between 400 and 750.[2] Because women registered for the service using male names, and a woman's true identity was not revealed unless she was injured or killed or she admitted it, getting an accurate count is difficult.

Choosing such an existence was not easy, but it offered opportunities for those who decided to take on the challenges. Faced with few rights as females, some women wanted to escape their everyday lives or poor situations at home. Joining the army also offered women an adventure and a chance to emulate the heroines they read about in popular books. At a time when women had few options outside of getting married and raising a family, many women enlisted in the army for the independence that came with being a man. Others wanted to be near husbands, brothers, fathers, or friends who were serving. Some working-class women signed up for a regular paycheck. Many regiments offered cash payments for soldiers who joined their ranks. But many women signed up for the same reasons men did—they truly believed in the Confederate or Union cause.

A SENSE OF COMPASSION

Upon discovering a fellow soldier was actually a woman, men often reacted with a sense of awe and compassion, even if the woman was fighting for the other side. Mark Nickerson, a Union private, remembered a sergeant in his regiment learning a female Confederate soldier was among the dead at the Battle of Antietam (September 17, 1862) in Maryland. Before she was buried in a separate grave, several soldiers went to see the woman soldier. The sight of her face brought tears to the eyes of many of the men.

RUNNING AWAY

For Edmonds, fighting in the war was the result of running away from home in search of a better life. Born in December 1841, Edmonds was the only child of a farmer from New Brunswick, Canada. Her father had always resented the fact that she was not a boy and had treated her badly all her life. In 1857, just before she was to enter into an arranged marriage to a man she despised, Edmonds ran away from home. She spent approximately a year working in Moncton, New Brunswick, before crossing the border into the United States.

Worried about traveling alone and being returned to her father's farm, Edmonds dressed like a man and adopted the name Franklin Thompson. Disguising herself as a man got Edmonds into the United States, where she got a job in Hartford, Connecticut, as a traveling Bible salesman. Eventually, she settled in Flint, Michigan, which is where she lived when the Civil War started. On May 25, 1861, she decided to join the Michigan infantry and enlisted for three years. Like many other women in the North at the time, Edmonds believed in the strength of the Union and had a strong desire to do something significant to help the war effort. "I could only thank God that I was free and could go forward and work, and I was not obliged to stay at home and weep," Edmonds said.[3]

Mary Ann Clark's tale is also one of running away. This resident of Kentucky joined the Confederate forces to escape the disappointment she felt when her husband left his family of four to marry a woman in California. Heartbroken, Clark left her son and daughter with her mother and headed off to fight under the alias Henry Clark.

NOT TO BE LEFT BEHIND

Other women, such as Frances Jamieson, joined the military to be near loved ones. After Jamieson's husband was killed at the First Battle of Bull Run, she left the regiment and became a nurse for the Hospital Corps. Without her husband by her side, she saw no reason to remain a soldier.

Frances Hook fought for the Union to remain close to her brother. The two siblings from Chicago, Illinois, had suffered through the deaths of their parents and were inseparable. When her brother enlisted, Hook did as well, using the name Frank Miller. She could not bear to be without him, especially as he was her only living relative. Hook continued

Fighting as men allowed some women to step outside their roles as wives and mothers.

INSPIRED BY HEROINES IN LITERATURE

Many of the Civil War memoirs penned by women soldiers reveal a common theme: these women were inspired by the brave female characters they read about in books. *Fanny Campbell, the Female Pirate Captain: A Tale of the Revolution!* gave Sarah Emma Edmonds the idea to dress as a man to escape her overbearing father. Loreta Janeta Velazquez drew inspiration from real-life heroines Molly Pitcher of the Revolutionary War (1775–1783) and Joan of Arc.

to serve after her brother died in the Battle of Shiloh (April 6–7, 1862). She reenlisted multiple times using a variety of aliases.

KEEPING THEIR SECRET

While passing herself as a man to fight as a soldier was relatively easy, any woman who did so lived in constant fear of being discovered. Numerous reports exist of women enduring extremely painful injuries because they did not want to go to a field hospital for treatment and risk revealing their true identities.

Edmonds is one woman who suffered for secrecy. She was injured three times and became ill with malaria as a soldier, but she always chose to treat these ailments herself rather than go to a field hospital and risk revealing her true identity. Later, as a veteran, she wrote a letter to the government asking for an increase in her pension to cover the cost of care related to her wartime injuries. The government refused, stating it had no proof she had ever been admitted to a hospital. In response, Edmonds wrote,

> *Had I been what I represented myself to be, I should have gone to a hospital. . . . But being a woman I felt compelled to suffer in silence . . . in*

MARY ELLEN WISE

In many instances, the government refused to pay military women, including Mary Ellen Wise. She served in the Thirty-Fourth Indiana Infantry as James Wise in September 1861. During a battle at Lookout Mountain in Chattanooga, Tennessee, Wise sustained a shoulder injury that could not be ignored. When a doctor discovered Wise was a woman, the army discharged her immediately. After recovering from her injury, Wise went to Washington, DC, and demanded payment for the time she had served. The paymaster refused to pay a woman for doing a soldier's work. President Lincoln heard about Wise's case in August 1864. He demanded Wise be paid. She received full payment for her time as a Union soldier. On September 30, 1874, Wise's story appeared in the pages of the *Washington Daily Morning Chronicle* in an article titled "Brave Soldier Girl."

order to escape detection of my sex. I would rather have been shot dead, than to have been known to be a woman and sent away from the army.[4]

Velazquez was injured during the war fighting for the South. She was shot in the foot while working as a scout in Tennessee, near Fort Donelson. Fearing doctors would discover her identity, she decided not to get medical help at the army's camp and went home to New Orleans, Louisiana, instead.

Jane Short's story reveals the consequences of being discovered. Short enlisted in the Union army under the name Charley Davis. She suffered an injury to her hand during the Battle of Shiloh. She did not seek medical treatment until later, when she became ill as a result of her wound. In the hospital, doctors

LORETA JANETA VELAZQUEZ

1842–1897?

Loreta Janeta Velazquez was born to a wealthy family in Cuba and grew up with an aunt in New Orleans. She married William, an American soldier, when she was a young teenager. The couple had two children and eventually moved to Saint Louis, Missouri. By 1860, both children had died of fever. Feeling alone and sad, Velazquez begged William to allow her to join him in fighting for the Confederate army. When he refused, Velazquez cut her hair, put on a soldier's uniform, took the name Harry T. Buford, and set out for Arkansas, where she gathered a regiment of 236 volunteer soldiers.[5] Velazquez and her regiment tracked down her husband with his regiment in Florida, where she introduced herself to him as her regiment's commanding officer. William was astonished. When William was killed in a gun accident, Velazquez left her regiment and traveled north on her own to meet up with Confederate troops at Bull Run. She fought with regiments until she feared she would be discovered, then moved on. She also fought in the Battles of Ball's Bluff, Fort Donelson, and Shiloh. During her storied military career, Velazquez spent time spying and was fined for impersonating a man. In 1876, she wrote *Women in Battle*, a memoir about her experiences as a Confederate soldier.

discovered her sex. They continued to treat Short, but the army discharged her immediately.

The women who wore a soldier's uniform and fought in battles during the Civil War showed tremendous bravery. Many other women demonstrated their bravery and dedication to the war effort in another way. They cared for the thousands of soldiers who became injured or ill during the war years.

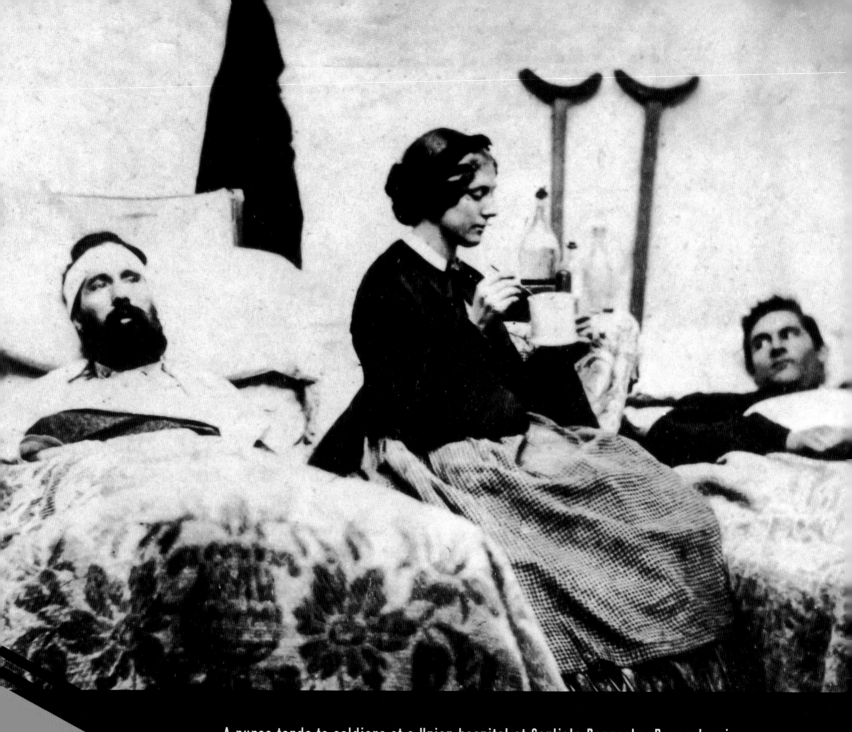

A nurse tends to soldiers at a Union hospital at Carlisle Barracks, Pennsylvania.

CHAPTER 4

TENDING THE WOUNDED

As the first casualties of war quickly filled hospitals throughout the North and the South, it became painfully clear medical facilities, doctors, and nurses were not prepared to treat thousands of new patients. When the war began, the North and the South had only 150 hospitals and no training programs for nurses.[1] Nearly all nurses at the time were men because society considered women too delicate for the difficult and often gruesome work.

A CALL FOR NURSES

A change in nursing came in 1862. In the summer of that year, as hospitals and other makeshift facilities became overcrowded with ill and injured soldiers, US Army surgeon general William Hammond invited women to apply to nursing positions. Initially, only women ages 35 to 50 would be accepted, but the age was later lowered to 30. Female nurses had to dress in plain brown, black, or gray clothing. They could wear none of the jewelry, lace, or other adornments that were fashionable at the time. The combination of age and plainness was intended to discourage romantic interest by soldiers in the nurses. Female nurses were paid twenty cents a day, plus rations. Male nurses, however, received twenty dollars per month and more benefits.[2]

When the call for female nurses went out, 2,000 women volunteered almost immediately. Six hundred trained nurses from Catholic orders reported for duty in 12 field hospitals located near front lines.[3] In the early years of the war, these new nurses were thrown into the fray, receiving training as they worked.

Author Louisa May Alcott volunteered for nursing duty at the Union Hotel, a makeshift hospital in Washington, DC, in December 1862. She got there just as Union soldiers hurt in the Battle of Fredericksburg on December 13 were arriving. She described her first day on the job in *Hospital Sketches*, one of the first memoirs about life as a nurse during the Civil War, published in August 1863:

> *There they were! "our brave boys," as the papers justly call them, for cowards could hardly have been so riddled with shot and shell, so torn and shattered, nor have borne suffering for which we have no name, with an uncomplaining*

fortitude. . . . In they came, some on stretchers, some in men's arms, some feebly staggering along propped on rude crutches, and one lay stark and still with covered face, as a comrade gave his name to be recorded before they carried him away to the dead house.[4]

BEING A NURSE

Civil War nurses responded to what was asked of them hour by hour. They made the rounds among soldiers, cleaning and bandaging wounds, changing bandages, and giving medicine to the ill. The flood of wounded after a battle made everyone work as quickly as possible to save as many lives as they could. Nurses also performed everyday housekeeping tasks, such as gathering and washing laundry and cooking meals. Perhaps one of the most important tasks on the Civil War nurse's to-do list was not officially part of the job description: these women befriended soldiers, comforted them, and kept them company. To pass the time, nurses would read to soldiers from favorite books or help them write letters to

HOSPITAL FOOD

By the time soldiers landed in the hospital, many had subsisted on a very limited diet for many months. Union soldiers consumed hardtack and coffee. Confederate soldiers had cornbread and chicory. Soldiers also ate salt pork or beef when available. This is why nurses baked goods for their charges whenever possible. Gingerbread was both delicious and easy for the soldiers to digest. Custards were favorite sweets as well. Fresh fruit was also very popular and was the treat President Lincoln and author Walt Whitman each brought when they visited hospitals. In his journal from the time, Whitman noted soldiers often requested horehound candy and rice pudding.

relatives. In the evenings, nurses would sometimes entertain troops by singing or playing music.

Nurses also sat with soldiers as they breathed their last breaths, holding their hands and offering words of comfort. Alcott wrote about sitting with a soldier named John Suhre as he was dying from a gunshot wound to one of his lungs. "He held my hand close," Alcott recalled, "so close that when he was asleep at last I could not draw it away."[5]

Many nurses were surprised by how quickly they became accustomed to seeing the horrific battle wounds soldiers endured. As Susie King Taylor, an African-American nurse who worked with Clara Barton, explained,

> It seems strange how our aversion to seeing suffering is overcome in war, how we are able to see the most sickening sights, such as men with their limbs blown off and mangled by the deadly shells, without a shudder, and instead

NUN NURSES

Hundreds of nurses who cared for soldiers during the Civil War were Catholic nuns. In 1863, they were among the only trained nurses in the country. They had knowledge acquired and recorded over generations as part of their orders' devotion to caring for the sick. By 1860, Catholic nuns managed 28 hospitals in America.[6]

Nuns from several orders served as nurses in the war. They worked on battlefields, in hospitals, and aboard ships. Edwin Stanton, the US secretary of war, specifically asked for the Sisters of Mercy, an order in Pittsburgh, Pennsylvania, to operate military hospitals in Pittsburgh and Washington, DC. In 1924, Congress honored the nun nurses of the Civil War with a monument in Washington, DC.

of turning away, how we hurry to assist in alleviating their pain, bind up their wounds, and press the cool water to their parched lips, with feelings only of sympathy and pity.[7]

IN HARM'S WAY

Although female nurses were common in hospitals during the war, few women were allowed to volunteer for the more dangerous job of field nurse, a nurse who tends to the wounded on the front lines. The job was not an easy one. A field nurse was in constant danger of being shot. During a battle, field nurses were often told to leave injured and dying soldiers where they lay until the fighting subsided. Often this meant denying treatment at

The magazine *Harper's Weekly* ran an image in 1862 depicting women in action during the war, including a nun nurse.

THE SISTER OF CHARITY

THE INFLUENCE

CLARA BARTON

1821–1912

When the first soldiers injured in the Civil War began filling the streets of Washington, DC, in 1861, Clara Barton came to their aid. A former schoolteacher from Massachusetts, Barton worked as a clerk for the US Patent Office. She immediately tried to help the soldiers, many of whom were hungry and had nothing but the clothes they wore. Barton gathered bedding, medical supplies, and food, delivering it to the Capitol building, where the Sixth Massachusetts Infantry had found shelter. Barton also read to the men, helped them write letters home, and listened to them.

Barton arranged to deliver wagons filled with supplies to field hospitals on the front lines. She earned the title "Angel of the Battlefield" for her ability to appear on the battlefield when supplies were most needed.[8] After the war, Barton contacted the families of missing prisoners of war to help them locate their loved ones. In 1881, inspired by a visit to the International Red Cross, a relief organization in Switzerland, Barton created a Red Cross chapter in the United States.

critical life-or-death moments, which was agonizing for field nurses to endure and witness.

But as circumstances unfolded on the battlefield, many women did whatever was needed to care for fallen soldiers, even if that meant taking on the role of field nurse. Elmina Spencer, who was with the 147th New York Regiment, was known to travel 30 to 40 miles (48 to 64 km) a day on horseback to gather much-needed medical supplies. At Gettysburg, Pennsylvania, Spencer rode ahead of the troops and set up camp in an abandoned barn, where she started a fire and began to boil water in anticipation of the influx of wounded soldiers. Instead, she got word that General John Reynolds, who led the regiment, had been killed, and the rebel troops were advancing her way. Rather than take the advice of the Union soldiers and retreat to safety, Spencer headed onto the battlefield. There, beneath the spray of gunfire, she began to tend to the wounded. At dusk, Spencer led a group of injured soldiers to a church on the Baltimore Pike, where they planned to set up a makeshift hospital. As the

ONE NURSE'S REALIZATION

Amanda Akin worked as a nurse at Armory Square Hospital in Washington, DC. On June 14, 1863, Akin wrote to her sister about a realization she had:

It seemed to me this evening, as I sat at my table adding to the list of medicines—writing down name, regiment, list of clothing, etc., of the new arrivals, calmly looking at the poor maimed sufferers carried by, some without limbs, on a 'stretcher'—that I had forgotten how to feel, . . . it seemed as if I were entirely separated from the world I had left behind.[9]

SPREAD OF DISEASE

Medical practices in place during the Civil War era ultimately led to the deaths of thousands of soldiers. The shortage of qualified doctors forced both sides to recruit inexperienced surgeons, many of whom had never treated a gunshot wound and did not know how to do surgery. These physicians learned on the job. Also, no one knew the importance of using sterile bandages and keeping clean. Doing both greatly reduces the spread of disease and the rates of infection after surgery. Doctors routinely neglected to clean and sterilize surgical tools between patients and often did not wash their hands because they did not have fresh water. In army camps, toilets were often dug too close to the streams used for drinking water, which promoted the spread of dysentery, the disease that killed the most soldiers during the war.

battle progressed, Spencer saved the life of a soldier who had been shot through the neck, even though others had given up on him. She also cared for 600 other Union soldiers, as well as 200 Confederate soldiers.[10] For her bravery and compassion in the face of danger, Spencer is listed on a Gettysburg monument dedicated to the 147th New York Regiment.

Anna Etheridge was also at Gettysburg. She was a nurse with Michigan's Third Corps. Known as "Gentle Annie," Etheridge rode through the battlefield in search of wounded soldiers.[11] She had loaded her saddlebags with lint and bandages, ready to treat soldiers in need. One officer from Pennsylvania saw Etheridge as she rode back from the front and remembered her grace under pressure: "She asked for some information, and quickly returned to the front again. She . . . was directing the removal of the wounded. She was cool and self-possessed and did not seem to mind the fire."[12] Over the course of the war, Etheridge nursed fallen soldiers in at least 32 battles. For her efforts, the US Army awarded Etheridge

Nurses and wounded soldiers at a hospital in Washington, DC, in 1865

the Kearny Cross, a medal honoring great bravery. She was one of only three women to receive it.

OCCUPATIONAL HAZARDS

Working in close quarters with ill soldiers put nurses at constant risk for getting sick themselves. Two out of three soldiers who died in the Civil War died

Nurses tend to wounded at a hospital established in the Union Hotel in

from disease, not battle wounds.[13] The most common diseases were dysentery, typhoid, yellow fever, malaria, smallpox, measles, tuberculosis, and pneumonia.

Alcott, for example, came down with typhoid pneumonia less than one month after reporting for duty as a nurse at the Union Hotel in Washington, DC. She resisted the disease at first, continuing to tend to soldiers despite a bad cough and high fever. Her supervisor, Hannah Ropes, finally forbid Alcott to leave her bed, where she kept busy knitting for the soldiers. Ropes wrote to Alcott's family, requesting they come and take Alcott home to recuperate. But it would take the death of Ropes herself two weeks later, on January 20, 1863, before Alcott agreed to go home.

The challenging work of caring for wounded soldiers—often with few supplies in unsanitary conditions—required compassionate, determined, and dedicated individuals. For those who tended soldiers in the South, shortages and destruction of property added hardship to an already difficult job.

An unidentified Southern woman with her husband, a Confederate soldier, and their baby

CONFEDERATE WOMEN'S WAR

With Union and Confederate troops fighting most of their battles on Southern soil, women in the South—black and white—often felt the effects of the war more acutely than Northern women, suffering both personal losses and everyday hardships. Under these difficult circumstances, women took on a more prominent role in Southern society, voicing their opinions on the war and doing whatever they could to help the war effort.

PRESSURING MEN TO ENLIST

As Southern states began withdrawing from the Union, elite white women openly voiced their support for secession. If slavery were to end, the social order of the South would be threatened. Many pressured their husbands, relatives, and friends to join the Confederate troops and fight for an independent South. If a boyfriend or husband talked of not enlisting, women would tell these men they were shirking their duty to the Confederacy.

Bowing to this pressure, men enlisted and marched off to battle, including those who had no desire to fight. Although Confederates had the advantages of strong devotion to the Southern cause and fighting the war on familiar territory, the odds were stacked against them. By the end of the war, for example, the Confederacy would send 880,000 soldiers off to battle compared with the North's 2.1 million.[1]

RUNNING THE FARM

With their men off fighting for the Confederacy, many Southern women were left to run small family farms, plantations, and households on their own. These women struggled to round up family

SMUGGLING MEDICINE FROM THE NORTH

At the beginning of the Civil War, the North established a naval blockade around the South. The North closed all Southern ports and captured or blocked all ships that tried to get through. Because most medicines were manufactured in the North, and the blockade prevented shipments from reaching Confederate troops, Southern women and children would sneak across Union lines to take medicines such as quinine and morphine. Women would stitch stolen bottles of medicine into their elaborate hoop skirts and smuggle them south of the Mason-Dixon Line, the boundary separating Maryland in the South from Pennsylvania in the North, delivering them to troops in the field along the way.

MARY CHESNUT

1823–1886

One of the many Southern women who kept a journal during the Civil War was Mary Boykin Miller Chesnut. Born in South Carolina to a politician father, Mary married a politician, James Chesnut Jr. when she was 17. James served as a US senator for South Carolina and left that job to help lead the state's secession. Later, he was an aide to Confederate president Jefferson Davis. During the war, James served different roles, including acting as commanding general of South Carolina's reserve forces.

Mary joined her husband on military missions during the war. She kept a diary from February 1861 to June 1865. Mary's husband was part of the negotiations at Fort Sumter in April 1861. She wrote about events on April 12: "The shells were bursting. . . . I knew my husband was rowing about in a boat somewhere in that dark bay, and that the shells were roofing it over, bursting toward the fort. If Anderson was obstinate, Colonel Chesnut was to order the fort on one side to open fire. Certainly fire had begun. . . . And who could tell what each volley accomplished of death and destruction?"[2]

Mary's journal was published in 1905 as *A Diary from Dixie*. Historians consider it a valuable primary source.

members and men who were not fighting to help on the farm and often did not have the animals, seeds, equipment, and other tools required to grow crops. During the war, a government policy called impressment allowed Confederate troops to take slaves, food, corn, firewood, fuel, and livestock. As the war dragged on and conditions worsened for the Confederacy, it was common for Southerners to pretend to be impressment agents in an attempt to gather food and supplies for their own destitute families.

Union and Confederate armies stripped farms located near Southern battlefields clean of supplies, and mortar fire damaged farmland beyond use, leaving women on the farms with no way to make a living. This problem affected much more than individual family farms. These same farms were the ones the Confederacy had been counting on to feed its soldiers and citizens. Instead of growing food for the Confederacy, farmhouses near battlefields often became makeshift hospitals where Southern women received on-the-job training in nursing.

GUERRILLA WARFARE

Southern families in rural areas throughout the Confederacy faced the constant threat of attack by guerrilla fighters, which Union troops called bushwhackers. During these raids, guerrillas from both sides of the conflict beat or killed any men who were on the property, threatened women and children with guns, and stole any food, fuel, firewood, or weapons they could find. Some young Southern women committed to the Confederate cause actually aided the guerrillas, gathering supplies and delivering them by wagon.

Wealthy white women left to run cotton plantations faced a slightly different problem. Despite the common perception that the Civil War South was a place where all white families owned plantations and all African Americans worked as slaves on those plantations, this is far from the truth. In reality, approximately 31 percent of white families in the Confederacy owned slaves.[3] Of these, 88 percent of slave owners had fewer than 20 slaves, and half had fewer than five slaves.[4] Fewer than 10,000 families owned more than 50 slaves, and fewer than 3,000 families owned more than 100 slaves.[5]

Although in many cases there were enough slaves remaining on their plantations to plant, tend, and harvest crops, with so many white plantation owners away at war, the mistress of the house was often forced to add supervision of the field slaves to her existing management of house slaves. For many women, this added responsibility was a source of endless frustration. Although Southern women may have been skilled at running a household of slaves, few had any training on how to run farm production or manage field workers. And some women wound up leading in the same manner as their male counterparts: forcefully. Some Southern women ordered violence against slaves.

Also, with the master away, many slaves refused to obey the mistress. As a result, production on many plantations slowed considerably. Instances of slaves stealing food, ignoring curfew, or leaving to visit friends or family on other plantations increased. In addition, more slaves attempted escape. As Union troops marched farther south, slaves ran away from plantations to Union camps.

Plantation mistresses sometimes fled their homes before the troops arrived, traveling deeper into the South to avoid the enemy. These Southern women became refugees and sought safety in neighboring Confederate states. Those who returned to their stately homes more often than not found them destroyed and looted by Union forces. Southern women prepared for such raids by hiding valuables such as fine silver and china under floorboards in the house and sneaking smaller valuables in pockets hidden under their hoop skirts.

RESOURCES: NORTH VERSUS SOUTH

The Southern disadvantage extended well beyond manpower. In 1860, the North far outpaced the South in manufacturing, which would become crucial during the war.

	NORTH	SOUTH
Weapons	97%	3%
Locomotives	96%	4%
Pig iron	93%	7%
Boots and shoes	90%	10%
Cloth	94%	6%[6]

FOOD RIOTS

The war quickly took its toll on women and children in the South. The Confederate government never anticipated running low on food. Because the South had plenty of farms, the government thought the South could grow enough fruits and vegetables to feed the soldiers and the families left at home. But the Confederates soon discovered destruction caused during battles often destroyed farmland. The South depleted its food sources within two years. Prices for food and other necessary goods more than doubled. At the same time, profiteers bought all the available goods from stores and sold them at much higher prices—prices few families could afford.

The Confederacy responded to the rising cost of goods by printing more money. This move did not help the situation. Instead, it caused the value of Confederate currency to plummet. By 1865, the Confederate dollar was worth one-sixtieth its original value.[7] This sent the price of food and other goods through the roof. In Richmond, Virginia, for example, a pound of bacon cost $1.25 in 1860 and $10 in February 1863.[8] Working-class Southern women became desperate. Surviving on the meager payments their soldier husbands sent home was extremely difficult. Many of these women had children to feed, taxes to pay to fund the war effort, and a farm to run. The amount of a Confederate soldier's paycheck did not increase to meet the increased cost of living.

Some women pleaded with Confederate government officials to help, but these pleas often went unanswered. Nancy Mangum of McLeanesville, North Carolina, wrote a letter to North Carolina governor Zebulon Vance:

> A crowd of we Poor wemen went to Greenesborough yesterday for something to eat as we had not a mouthful meet nor bread in my house. What did they do but put us in gail. . . . I have 6 little children and my husband in the armey and

The Confederacy printed its own currency, but increasing production did not help the situation when the cost of goods increased.

what am I to do . . . if you don't take thes yankys a way from greenesborough

we wemen will write for our husbans to come . . . home and help us.[9]

Some women begged storekeepers for food. Finally, 1,000 women in Richmond resorted to raiding stores for food and supplies on April 2, 1863.[10] A similar riot took place in Mobile, Alabama, on September 4, 1863, when a crowd of angry women took to the streets with axes, hammers, and brooms. In what became known as the bread riots, women decided they had no choice but to steal the food they could not afford to buy.

DEVOTED TO THE CONFEDERACY

Despite the food shortages, destruction of property, and chaos that sometimes occurred, Southern women endured. Many remained outspoken about their loyalty to the Confederacy throughout the war. After her family's plantation home in Baton Rouge, Louisiana, was ransacked by Union soldiers in August 1862, Sarah Morgan felt a renewed sense of allegiance to the Confederacy:

> I have lost my home and all its dear contents for our Southern Rights, have stood on its deserted hearthstone and looked at the ruin of all I loved—without a murmur, almost glad of the sacrifice it would contribute its mite towards the salvation of the Confederacy.[11]

CONFEDERATE DESERTERS

As Confederate soldiers on the front lines received word their families were suffering, many felt a sense of helplessness. Their wives and children were going hungry or were unable to buy proper clothing or shoes. Some families were at risk for being kicked out of homes or farms because they did not have enough money to pay rent. James Seddon, secretary of war for the Confederacy, reported one-third of the Confederate army had abandoned the battlefields and headed for home by November 1863 to help their struggling families. Some scholars argue women encouraged men to desert.

This artwork shows Southern women encouraging their men to fight and then, later when times are desperate, rioting for much needed food.

In addition to declaring their support for their new nation, elite white women in the Confederacy also were not shy about showing their disrespect and disdain for the Union soldiers who occupied Southern cities. Women openly taunted Union soldiers, ignored their commands, and crossed the street to avoid passing them on the sidewalk. In Union-held cities and towns, Southern women were required to recite an oath of loyalty to the Union. Those who refused could not enter Union-held cities or conduct business in city establishments. Morgan wrote in her diary that she and her mother refused to recite the oath aloud when they arrived in Union-occupied New Orleans: "I confess myself a rebel, body and soul. *Confess?* I glory in it! Am proud of being one; would not forego the title for any other earthly one."[12]

Morgan was fervently devoted to the Confederate cause. For the first half of the war, many Northern women did not have a unifying cause to rally behind. That would change when Lincoln announced the Emancipation Proclamation on September 22, 1862.

Female students in Philadelphia, Pennsylvania, sew a US flag in the 1860s.

CHAPTER ★ 6 ★

WOMEN IN THE NORTH

As Northern men marched off to join the Union army, Northern women began to take a more active role in politics. At a time when females had few rights of their own—they could not vote, going to college was frowned upon, and job opportunities were limited—fighting for the rights of slaves resonated for some women. Other women were content simply to express an opinion about the war. In the mid-1800s, when women were not supposed to have opinions about politics, let alone talk about them, this was a pivotal shift in the way women viewed their role in society.

Empowered with a new sense of civic duty, Northern women began to follow the lead of Harriet Beecher Stowe. Some Northern women got their first real glimpse of what slavery might be like from reading Stowe's story about the life of a slave. While slavery was at the core of the Civil War, many Americans did not have direct experience with the practice. The *National Era*, an antislavery magazine, published Stowe's story in segments between June 5, 1851, and April 1, 1852. An estimated 50,000 people nationwide eagerly awaited each installment.[1] By the time the installments were published in book form as *Uncle Tom's Cabin* in March 1852, an antislavery sentiment had captured the minds and hearts of many Northerners and even some abolitionists in the South. In fact, the book took the United States by storm. *Uncle Tom's Cabin* became the best-selling book of the 1800s, second only to the Bible.

HARRIET BEECHER STOWE

Author and abolitionist Harriet Beecher Stowe was born on June 14, 1811, in Litchfield, Connecticut. When her family moved to Cincinnati, Ohio, in 1832, a city just across the Ohio River from the slave state of Kentucky, 21-year-old Harriet met many fugitive slaves and witnessed slavery firsthand. After Stowe married and had a family of her own, she and her husband employed fugitives in their home. When the family learned one of their servants was a runaway slave, Stowe's husband helped the young girl escape to Canada. After the Fugitive Slave Act was passed in 1850, Stowe complained about the injustice of slavery to her sister-in-law, Isabella Porter Beecher, who encouraged Stowe to write about her experiences. She did.

Uncle Tom's Cabin, chronicling the life of a slave, was published in 1852 and read by millions. When President Lincoln met Stowe in Washington, DC, during the Civil War, legend has it he said, "So you are the little woman who wrote the book that started this great war."[2]

Yet just before the Civil War erupted in April 1861, Lincoln made it clear the Union was not fighting to end slavery in the South. In the president's inaugural address on March 4, 1861, he told Americans he would not abolish slavery where it already existed. He also had no plans to repeal the Fugitive Slave Act of 1850, which granted local governments the authority to capture and return runaway slaves to their owners. Instead, the North was fighting the war in an attempt to restore the Union to what it had been before the Confederate states seceded. This did not please abolitionists, free blacks, and slaves, who longed to see slavery put to rest once and for all.

GETTING POLITICAL

Northern women found inspiration in Stowe. Just as she had expressed her antislavery opinion in her writing, they found the courage to state their opinions on the political issues of the day. Many women, especially those who had been abolitionists before the war, were not afraid to speak out against the president when he appeared to drag his feet on the subject of emancipation. Women spoke out in public, in published articles, and in letters sent directly to the president. For example, when Lincoln removed General John C. Fremont from command in Missouri after Fremont declared martial law in the state and announced the slaves of all those who were disloyal to the US government would be freed, women responded. Mrs. E. A. Spaulding of Connecticut wrote to the president,

"When it becomes necessary for a female, a weak insignificant female in view of the times to lift up her voice in defence of right, it most conclusively proves that there is an existing wrong."[3]

Some women did their part to proclaim the many evils of slavery whenever Lincoln seemed to waver on the issue. When asked to speak at the Capitol on January 16, 1864, young abolitionist and orator Anna Dickinson reportedly criticized the president harshly to the audience, which included the country's top Republicans—even Lincoln. The Women's National Loyal League took the role of government watchdog. The group supported the president when his policies

Harriet Beecher Stowe inspired many Northern women to fight for an end to slavery.

worked toward abolishing slavery and criticized him when he seemed to step in the other direction.

BOOMING ECONOMY

While Northern women found their voices in a way similar to their counterparts in the South, the two groups had very different economic experiences. As women in the South suffered extreme shortages and hardships, industry in the North boomed. Coal and iron production soared as both were needed for the war effort. Overseas trade reached an all-time high, and traffic on Northern railroads increased by 50 percent.[4] As business prospered, Northern investors and entrepreneurs became rich seemingly overnight. Many were criticized for flaunting their wealth by building extravagant mansions and dressing in expensive clothing while Union soldiers died on battlefields far from home.

Some of the North's new prosperity did trickle down to the working class in the form of jobs, but wages did not

THE NORTHERN ELITE

As working-class white Northerners worked overtime to put food on the table, the lives of Northern elite women changed very little during the war. In fact, when their husbands profited handsomely from wartime industry in the North, most of these women enjoyed more wealth than they had before the war began. Society women in the North continued to attend parties and balls, wearing elaborate gowns made from the finest silk and expensive jewelry made with precious gems. Women of means made monetary donations to the war effort and attended benefits and fund-raising fairs.

keep pace with inflation. That left some families barely able to get by. But, with so many men away fighting the war, opportunities arose for women in the workplace, especially in manufacturing. Approximately 300,000 women joined the workforce during the Civil War.[5] Before the war, women held one-quarter of the manufacturing jobs. During the war, they held one-third.[6] Openings for jobs that were traditionally filled by women were abundant, including textile work, shoemaking, and teaching. Women also had the chance to try a few higher-paying jobs that usually went to men, such as artillery manufacturing, mill work, government clerkships, and farming.

Many young, unmarried women chose to leave home to support the war effort. The most popular destination was Washington, DC. There, they hoped to find a position as a nurse at one of several hospitals that had been hastily opened to accommodate the influx of injured soldiers. Other women traveled south into Union-held Southern areas to teach freed slaves to read and write.

WORKING FOR THE UNION TROOPS

Approximately 20,000 working-class white women and free and former slave African-American women found work with the Union armies.[7] These women traveled with the regiments, doing laundry, cooking, sewing and repairing clothing, tending to wounded soldiers, and performing other domestic tasks as needed. Women also tended gardens, growing food to prepare for the soldiers.

ADJUSTMENTS AT HOME

Although an estimated 70 percent of the soldiers in the Union army were not married, their absence left a big hole for many women in the North to fill.[8] Most soldiers were middle or working class and, usually, earned much of their families' income. Without those earnings, women and families struggled to make ends meet.

By 1863, middle- and working-class families began running low on money. "You had better send a little something to keep the family going," Elizabeth Ingersoll Fisher of Philadelphia wrote to her husband who was away in New York in September 1864.[9]

Some women moved in with relatives or friends to save the cost of housing and to pool limited resources. Emily Cox, another Pennsylvanian, had married Alexander Hensley, a soldier in the First Troop Philadelphia City Cavalry, in 1863. She decided to move in with her widowed mother. Rent was cheap at eight dollars a month, and she would be close to friends.[10] Living together would also keep both women from living alone.

SENDING MONEY HOME

As the war entered its second and third years, letters to soldiers from home were filled with continual pleas for money. Inflation and food shortages due to the war made food unaffordable. On the home front, women worried about feeding their children and became more and more desperate for money to pay for everyday necessities. Some regiments responded to these pleas by arranging to have a portion of soldiers' earnings sent directly home to help families. Massachusetts soldiers alone provided more than $3 million for their families via this method.[11]

LOW MORALE

By fall 1862, enthusiasm for the war was beginning to wane across the North. After Union troops suffered heavy losses at the Second Battle of Bull Run (August 28–30, 1862), Lincoln announced 300,000 more soldiers were needed on the front lines.[12] Few wanted to volunteer, especially working-class soldiers who were angry about a provision in the draft law that allowed the elite to buy their way out of military service. Civilians in Indiana, Ohio, Pennsylvania, and Wisconsin resisted, taking to the streets and threatening to riot. Union troops had to be brought in to quell the violence.

Northern women, who at the beginning of the war had quickly formed aid societies to address soldiers' needs for hats, mittens, gloves, bandages, food, and medical supplies, had become frustrated with a war that had already gone on longer than expected. Many soldiers had been lost, more from illness than battle, and

US SANITARY COMMISSION

When the Civil War began, hospitals tended to be dirty, chaotic places where germs and disease thrived. Little was known about the connection between germs and infection. To address the poor conditions in the Union army camps and hospitals, Henry Whitney Bellows and Dorothea Dix, the superintendent of the US Army Nurses, formed the US Sanitary Commission. The commission, which the federal government sanctioned in June 1861, raised money for medical supplies and recruited nurses, doctors, and volunteers to staff field hospitals. The commission also worked to educate Americans about the importance of cleanliness in warding off the spread of disease.

The US Sanitary Commission set up facilities near battlefields.

many more emerged from the war as amputees. Watching these men come home was not easy.

Relief efforts also disheartened women. Too many times, they heard from family members and friends fighting at the front who had not received their packages. The creation of the US Sanitary Commission in June 1861 addressed this issue somewhat by establishing a formal process for delivering care packages. But the commission also took a bit of the joy out of the relief effort by urging women to send general care packages to the troops instead of personalized ones for local regiments. Without a specific friend or family member to knit for, some women stopped knitting and sewing for the war effort altogether.

NORTHERN WOMEN'S PATRIOTISM

Northern soldiers made note of the strong sense of patriotism they witnessed among Southern women and wished Northern women showed the same dedication to their troops. Before long, the media began pointing fingers at Northern women for their lack of patriotism. One writer for the *New York Herald* wrote,

> But for the courage and energy of the women of the South, we believe the Rebellion would not have survived to this time. Had the women of the North with like zeal addressed themselves to the work of encouraging a loyal and devoted spirit among us, [the Union would have been more successful].[13]

Northern women, some people claimed, were not doing whatever they could to support the war effort. They were not writing enough letters. They were not sending enough handmade sweaters or enough canned goods. But what was really lacking among Northern women was an unwavering belief in the Union objective, which at that point remained simply bringing the secessionist states back into the fold. It was also difficult, with the war being fought on battlefields hundreds of miles away, for Northern women not to feel helpless and removed from the conflict, especially as more men died and the end was nowhere in sight.

This 1865 illustration shows one artist's hope for African Americans' future upon being freed by the Emancipation Proclamation.

EMANCIPATION PROCLAMATION

The weary spirit of Northern women finally got a long-awaited boost on January 1, 1863. On this day, Lincoln's administration finally issued the Emancipation Proclamation, a document stating slaves living in secession states

In addition to freeing slaves with the Emancipation Proclamation, Lincoln also made it possible for freed slaves to join the Union military.

would be free. This document shifted the Northern objective for the war from simply restoring the Union to abolishing slavery. It also renewed some women's faith in the government.

A letter by Rhonda Southworth to her son, who was a soldier for the Union, reflects the sense of optimism the government's actions inspired: "I am willing to make sacrifices for our beloved country, and now since we are taking steps in the right direction, I feel anxious to do what I can to advance the cause of freedom."[14]

e who

AFRICAN-AMERICAN WOMEN

Although the dawn of the Civil War ignited a spark of hope among African-American men and women who were enslaved in the South, a long, difficult journey to freedom still remained. During the early years of the war, those who escaped faced being captured and returned to their owners under the Fugitive Slave Act of 1850. They were not free—not yet.

ESCAPING TO FREEDOM

As Northern troops marched into border states, such as Tennessee and Virginia, some slaves in those Union-held territories escaped to freedom across Union lines. Unlike on plantations farther south, where the slaves most likely to attempt escape were male, in border states, women, children, and elderly slaves were also willing to take the risk. With a shorter distance to travel to freedom—only a few hours, instead of days—the possibility of actually succeeding seemed more likely. Many of those who fled left with nothing but the clothes they were wearing. They usually set out under cover of darkness and walked through the night, carrying a little food to make it through the first night of their journey. As they moved through the countryside, they lived in constant fear of being discovered. In an effort to avoid being seen, fugitives slept in tall grasses or heavily wooded areas, hiding until nightfall. Sometimes, runaway slaves walked along the edges of rivers and streams to avoid leaving a scent on land for dogs to follow.

Some slaves heading North in search of freedom had help along the way. Fugitives using the Underground Railroad usually traveled 10 to 20 miles (16 to 32 km) between stops. Hidden in a barn, attic, or crawl space to avoid detection, the fugitives would rest and eat before moving on the next night.

The people who helped fugitives along the way were called conductors. Harriet Tubman, a free African American living in Auburn, New York, who had escaped from slavery herself, was one of the most well-known conductors. In the 11 years before the Civil War, Tubman is believed to have made 19 trips south to help slaves to freedom. Tubman relied upon connections she had made through the Underground Railroad to lead 70 slaves north from Maryland. She helped another 60 or so make their way to Canada.[1]

Tubman also helped slaves in conjunction with Union forces. On June 2, 1863, she traveled up the Combahee River in South Carolina with Colonel James Montgomery and his troops. The soldiers attacked plantations as they moved upriver, liberating more than 700 slaves along the way.[2] Freed slaves escaped with what they could, from children to food to animals.

Escaping was only the beginning of the journey to freedom. Once an escaped slave arrived in the North with the help of the Underground Railroad, abolitionist organizations provided him or her with

Harriet Tubman's dedication to fighting slavery helped hundreds of enslaved African Americans gain freedom.

FACING PREJUDICE IN THE NORTH

When freed slaves arrived in the North, they faced a new challenge. Not all Northerners welcomed the newcomers with open arms. Prejudices about former slaves, including the idea that African Americans lacked intelligence and were dependent and lazy, permeated Northern thinking.

Many Northern women expressed concern that, without work, African Americans would live off government aid. As Northerner Clara Wood stated in a letter to her husband, "I should think it would be amusing to see those Darkies, you say they have a lot of Babies. I do hope they will not *increase* any faster now the Government provides for them."[3]

food, clean clothes, a place to live, and help finding a job. Those who escaped on their own later in the war, however, did not always have people waiting on the other side to help them.

CONTRABAND CAMPS

Without food or a place to stay, and with no way to make a living, fugitive African Americans began congregating around Union regiment camps in border states, hoping to find work with the army. The newly free men volunteered to fight for the Union. The women offered to do soldiers' laundry, mend uniforms and socks, and nurse the wounded. Some women took on backbreaking construction work on military fortifications.

As the number of runaway slaves increased, General Ulysses S. Grant, commander of the Union armies, saw the need to establish settlements where fugitive African Americans could live temporarily. In November 1862, Grant opened the first of such camps in Grand Junction, Tennessee. These camps, referred to as "contraband camps," were named after the "contraband" slaves who lived in them.[4] *Contraband*, which means goods that have been imported or exported illegally, described slaves who had escaped from the South to Union lines. By law, escaped slaves could not be returned to slave owners in the South. But the contraband slaves were not free, either, leaving them in a gray area between slavery and freedom. Camp refugees received care and a place to stay until they were able to find work and get back on their feet. Over the course of the war, Union troops would manage 100 contraband camps throughout the South.[5]

Conditions in many of the camps were very poor. Refugees often built their own ramshackle shelters out of whatever they could find. The camps quickly earned a reputation for breeding disease and illnesses, which spread quickly in the crowded conditions and claimed the lives of 1 million of the 4 million slaves freed during the Civil War.[6] In fact, some runaway slaves stayed away from the camps after hearing about the difficult living conditions and high mortality rates.

Women in the camps seldom had enough food and did not have adequate clothing or blankets to keep their families warm during the winter. In some more established camps, the federal government allowed women residents to grow their own food and raise animals on surrounding land that had been taken from the Confederacy. Women used the food they grew to cook meals and bake sweets,

CORINTH CONTRABAND CAMP

The Corinth Contraband Camp near Shiloh, Tennessee, was a camp success story. Established by Union general Grenville M. Dodge in 1863, Corinth consisted of well-constructed homes, a school, a hospital, and a church. Men and women worked in nearby fields, growing cotton and vegetables as part of a cooperative farm program, then sold the harvest for profit. Children attended school, where they learned to read and write. Through the services and support provided at Corinth, more than 1,000 adults and children learned to read.[7]

which they often sold to Union soldiers who had grown tired of living on mostly hardtack and coffee.

The challenge of how to accommodate the increasing numbers of runaway slaves in the North contributed to Lincoln's decision to draft the Emancipation Proclamation. As contraband camps filled beyond capacity, conditions deteriorated, and numerous African Americans began to die from disease. The Union faced a mounting social crisis. Life in most of the camps was not freedom—it was another kind of enslavement.

CONTRIBUTIONS BY FREE AFRICAN-AMERICAN WOMEN

As the war stretched on, the plight of the people in the contraband camps caught the attention of African-American women's aid organizations in the North. Such groups included the Chicago Colored Ladies' Freedmen's Aid Society and the Contraband Relief Associations in Washington, DC, and Boston. These organizations gathered essential goods, such as woolen clothing, food, and soap,

A memorial to the freed slaves at Corinth Contraband Camp includes a statue of an African-American woman ironing soldiers' uniforms.

and delivered care packages to the camps. Northern black women who had once been slaves, such as Sojourner Truth and Harriet Jacobs, traveled to the camps to help care for the refugees.

Women from Northern aid groups and Christian organizations also volunteered to teach African Americans in the camps to read and write. These skills would give these former slaves access to better employment opportunities in the North. Mary S. Peake was one of the first African-American women hired by the American Missionary Association to teach in a contraband camp near Fort Monroe in Hampton, Virginia. Although teaching slaves to read and write was illegal in Virginia, Peake quietly began meeting with small groups of six or seven contraband children under a big oak tree on September 17, 1861. A week later, it became increasingly difficult to keep the classes a secret as 50 or 60 children began attending each day.[8] The children learned to read quickly. Soon, adults showed an interest in learning themselves. Peake started a class for approximately 20 adults that met in the evenings.[9] The site where Peake taught these former slaves to read is now home to Hampton University, a major historically black college.

African-American women, including Tubman and Susie King Taylor, also served as nurses during the war. Tubman traveled to South Carolina in 1862 to volunteer as a nurse for the Union army. She dedicated her time to caring for black soldiers and freed slaves. Taylor, who was a slave until the age of 14, went to war with her husband, a soldier with the Thirty-Third US Colored Troops. She cared for wounded soldiers and did laundry for the regiment. Taylor also kept a detailed diary of her experiences on the front. It is the only surviving record of the war from the viewpoint of an African-American nurse.

Tubman and many other African-American women also served the Union as spies during the war. Mary Elizabeth Bowser had a job in the White House of the Confederacy, which was in Richmond. Bowser convinced her employer she could not read or write, and then used her photographic memory to gather and report top-secret information about the Confederate

Mary S. Peake's work as a teacher changed the lives of countless people.

SUSIE KING TAYLOR

1848–1912

Susie Baker was born into slavery in Liberty County, Georgia, on August 6, 1848. The year she turned seven, Susie was sent to live with her grandmother in Savannah, Georgia, where she attended secret schools for black children and learned to read and write. In April 1862, she was one of many African Americans who ran away to Saint Simons Island, which had recently been taken over by Union forces. When Union officers realized Susie could read and write, they asked if she could set up a school to teach the other African Americans on the island. She agreed. Soon, she had a classroom of 40 children each day in what was the first school for free blacks in Georgia.[10]

While on the island, Susie met and married a black officer named Edward King. She traveled with him during the war, helping as a nurse and laundress to his regiment. She taught several black soldiers to read and write as well. In 1866, Susie moved with her husband to Savannah, where she began a school for free black children. Her husband died that year. In 1867, Susie opened a school in Liberty County. Susie traveled to Boston, Massachusetts, in the 1870s with a white family for whom she worked as a servant. During the trip, she met Russell Taylor. The couple married. In 1902, she wrote the memoir *Reminiscences*. It is the only record of an African-American nurse's experiences during the Civil War. Susie died in Boston in 1912.

government for the Union. Many other women and men who had recently escaped slavery volunteered to spy for the Union. Former slaves easily slipped back into Confederate states, secured jobs as servants, and blended into the background at important meetings with the purpose of gathering information for the Union. African-American spies gave the Union a huge advantage during the war, allowing Union troops to gain the upper hand and eventually force the Confederacy to surrender.

WOMEN IN MOURNING

When the South finally surrendered at Appomattox Court House in Virginia on April 9, 1865, women in the North and South alike felt an overwhelming sense of relief. While most Southern women were disheartened by the outcome, everyone was weary of the death, destruction, and hardships the war had inflicted on both sides. In Northern cities and towns, Unionists filled the streets in celebration as soon as they heard the long war was finally over.

On April 15, however, the jubilant mood across the North came to an abrupt halt with the shocking news of Lincoln's death. He had been assassinated. The news threw the Union into shock and grief, especially Northern women, who had great faith in the president.

Mary Briggs Brooke of Sandy Spring, Maryland, wrote about the reaction in her diary:

FEMALE SOLDIERS RETURN HOME

After the war, women who served as soldiers for both sides often returned home quietly, without a hero's welcome. Many resumed the domestic lives typical of women of the time, and many did not reveal their military service until they were much older. This meant these women gave up any chance of receiving a pension for their years of service. As an older woman, Sarah Emma Edmonds appealed to Congress to pay her a pension. After gathering recommendations from fellow soldiers with whom she had served, Congress agreed to pay her a sum of $12 per month from that point forward.[2]

A sad day of absorbing interest and distress, we cannot withdraw our minds one moment from the shocking calamity which has burst so suddenly upon us. . . . In Washington, the whole City was draped in mourning, every yard of black material in all the stores, was sold out to furnish it, all business was stopped & men walked the streets in tears. . . . Johnson was inaugurated yesterday. I hope & trust he may fill the responsible office of Chief Magistrate better than has been feared.[1]

Brooke spoke for many Northern women and Unionists who wondered how the country would rebuild without Lincoln's leadership.

With so many soldiers missing and assumed dead, it is no surprise Northern and Unionist women reacted with such emotion to Lincoln's funeral. Seeing the president's casket gave these women a chance to mourn not only the president but their own loved ones who had gone missing or perished during the war.

Confederate sympathizers held a different view. Like Brooke, Margaret "Madge" Preston of Pleasant Plains, Maryland, kept a diary. The Southerner's entry on April 15, 1865, concerned Lincoln's assassination:

> *At eleven I sent Thede & Johnny to the city to bring Mr. Preston home, but owing to a joyful circumstance for this country, they were not able to get in, consequently returned bringing me the good news. It seems President Lincoln was assassinated last night at the Theatre in Washington and as poor Baltimore must be punished and suspected for doing all the wrong that is done the government, the authorities placed a guard round the city and will not let anyone in or out of the city without a pass.*[3]

From these two completely opposing viewpoints, which represented the general sentiment of the two regions, the United States was left to rebuild. But many women, whether they were from the North or South, faced the same heartbreaking, uphill battle in the years ahead. Everyone had to find a way to go on without the 750,000 husbands, sons, fathers, brothers, sisters, or friends who had died in the war.[4]

TAKING TIME TO MOURN

In the months immediately following the war, many families still did not know if loved ones had survived or died in battle. Of the hundreds of thousands of soldiers who lost their lives in the war, 40 percent were never identified.[5]

PHOTOJOURNALISM
HONORING THE DEAD

Before the invention of photography, families that could afford to hire an artist often honored their deceased loved ones by commissioning a painting of the departed. The development of photography technology in the 1840s led to the use of photos for this purpose instead. By the 1860s, this practice, known as post-mortem photography and mourning photography, had become quite popular.

For their portraits, the dead were sometimes propped in a chair or surrounded by grieving family members. Early mourning photographs usually were close-up shots. Making the person appear to be napping or even alive was common. For example, a dead child might be placed in a crib or shown with a toy. The child might also be photographed with his or her mother. Many photographers would hand paint the eyelids on such photos to make the dead look alive. Later, though, imagery changed to show the deceased person in a coffin. But the bodies of many soldiers were never recovered or were too badly damaged in battle to be photographed. Instead, family members posed for portraits while holding a photo of the deceased. In this image, a woman believed to be the wife of Confederate soldier James Shields wears a mourning dress and brooch containing a snapshot of her deceased husband. Her young child sits on her lap, wearing a soldier's cap.

At the end of the war, Clara Barton established the office of Missing Men of the United States Army, based in Washington, DC. As word spread that Barton was helping families track down missing soldiers, women throughout the North began writing to ask about their loved ones. Over the next three years, Barton received more than 68,000 letters.[6] She was able to find information on the whereabouts of 22,000 soldiers.[7]

PICKING UP THE PIECES

The soldiers who did return home were forever changed by their wartime experiences. Many who served had life-altering physical scars. One in 13 soldiers who survived the war was missing an arm or a leg.[8] Mothers, sisters, or wives of men with amputations found themselves in the new roles of caregiver and nurse. In many instances, the income lost when those soldiers left for the war was never regained. The majority of the soldiers came from working-class families with jobs in farming or industry, making returning to work difficult or impossible. This meant women were also the primary breadwinners. With wartime industries shutting down and able veterans returning to work, fewer jobs were available for women. Families of Union veterans received a monthly pension of between $8 and $20 per month from the federal government.[9] Families of Confederate veterans did not get a pension until the 1930s. Often, the payments were not enough to support a family, leaving many hungry and destitute.

A sign from
missing Civ

Other soldiers suffered emotionally and psychologically. Witnessing the death of friends or relatives on a daily basis takes a toll on a person's emotional well-being. Women were urged to provide comfort and to do whatever they could to help veterans ease back into civilian life.

For some soldiers, returning home brought back painful memories of how things used to be. Confederate soldiers, who sometimes encountered total destruction on the home front, felt this most acutely. Some of these soldiers decided to move their families West, where they could buy land and start a new life.

WOMAN'S RELIEF CORPS

Just as women had joined together in aid organizations to help soldiers during the war years, they organized local chapters of the Woman's Relief Corps (WRC) to provide support to Civil War veterans. Women began founding WRC chapters in 1882. By 1900, approximately 3,000 of these groups existed across the North and South. Membership totaled almost 120,000 and included white and African-American women.[10]

Each chapter of the WRC was established to serve a specific men's veterans group, usually a chapter of the Grand Army of the Republic, an organization for men who served in the Union forces. The WRC played a key role in Memorial Day ceremonies to honor Union soldiers who had lost their lives in the war.

The women decorated graves with flowers and flags and arranged for local schoolchildren to read poems and perform plays. Through these efforts, women of the WRC provided veterans with a place to reflect on the war and remember lost comrades.

The WRC also worked to promote patriotism in American schools. As a result of the efforts of WRC women, schoolchildren began reciting the Pledge of Allegiance and singing "The Star Spangled Banner," the national anthem, in school.

Although WRC groups originally formed to honor male soldiers, they eventually recognized the wartime contributions and sacrifices of women as

This 1910 illustration features a member of the Woman's Relief Corps.

well. "Let us remember that from the soldier alone came not all the sacrifice," explained the WRC president, Florence Barker, in 1884. "Many a brave woman's duty in the hospital—yes in the march and in the field—would compare in deeds of valor with that of the soldier."[11]

BACK IN HER PLACE

Having achieved the goal of ending slavery, women abolitionists were the first group to lead the battle for equal rights for women. Many women on both sides of the Civil War had grown accustomed to giving their opinions while men were away at war. As men returned from the front lines, however, women were expected to retreat to the domestic sphere, focusing again on cleaning house and rearing children. Most important, women were to return to the roles of quiet, subservient wives, mothers, daughters, and sisters. Women who spoke out were not taken seriously. Instead, they often were chastised for their "unwomanly behavior."[12]

But the Civil War gave women a taste of taking action. Whether they were making or gathering supplies to send to their troops, pushing for abolition, or helping newly freed slaves, women learned firsthand how to organize, manage, and do outreach for a cause. Women also felt the sense of empowerment that came from expressing their opinions. By war's end, however, it was clear women were still second-class citizens with few rights.

The Civil War was a defining moment in the lives of American women. It opened up new opportunities. For some, it was freedom. For others, it was a job or a vocation, such as nursing. Still others became leaders, focusing on a cause they found important. In the process, these women stepped out of the shadows of men, and they would continue to fight for equal status. This progress became the foundation upon which women continued to build the case for equal rights for all Americans, regardless of sex.

THE LOST CAUSE

During and following the war, Southern women worked to honor those who had perished. In Columbus, Georgia, women tended soldiers' graves. Columbus resident Lizzie Rutherford suggested a yearly observance when people would decorate the graves. Some people believe her idea is the source of Confederate Memorial Day. Celebrated on April 26, it recognizes soldiers who fought in the Civil War. This and other efforts to commemorate the fallen became an important part of Southern life and contributed to a form of cultural faith known as the Lost Cause. The Lost Cause takes an alternative, inaccurate view of the South and the Civil War. Rather than fighting to maintain slavery, Confederates were fighting to uphold the prewar Old South, which Southerners believed was refined and dignified. According to the Lost Cause, Confederates were simply standing up for themselves against the hostile and greedy Northerners, who invaded the South because they wanted to control the region. Southerners used this distorted view of history to reestablish white supremacy and justify horrible acts against blacks, such as lynching.

TIMELINE

November 1860

Abraham Lincoln, who is against slavery, is elected president of the United States.

December 20, 1860

South Carolina becomes the first state to secede from the United States.

February 1861

More states secede and form the Confederate States of America.

March 4, 1861

In his inaugural address, Lincoln states he has no plans to abolish slavery.

Summer 1862

William Hammond, surgeon general of the US Army, issues the first call for women nurses; 2,000 women apply.

August 1862

The Union suffers heavy losses at the Second Battle of Bull Run. Lincoln calls for more soldiers.

September 22, 1862

The Emancipation Proclamation is announced.

November 1862

In Grand Junction, Tennessee, General Ulysses S. Grant opens the first contraband camp.

April 12, 1861

Confederate troops attack Fort Sumter in South Carolina, igniting the Civil War.

April 15, 1861

The first Northern women's aid society forms in Bridgeport, Connecticut.

June 1861

The US Sanitary Commission forms.

July 21, 1861

Six women disguised as men fight in the first major battle of the Civil War, the First Battle of Bull Run.

January 1, 1863

The Emancipation Proclamation takes effect, freeing all slaves in states that seceded from the Union.

June 2, 1863

Harriet Tubman helps Union troops free 700 slaves in South Carolina.

April 9, 1865

The Confederacy surrenders to the Union at Appomattox Court House in Virginia.

1882

Women begin founding Women's Relief Corps chapters.

ESSENTIAL FACTS

KEY PLAYERS

- Clara Barton, who was known as the "Angel of the Battlefield," tirelessly gathered and delivered bedding, medical supplies, clothing, and food for Union soldiers during the war. In 1882, Barton created the first Red Cross chapter in the United States.

- Sojourner Truth was a former slave and abolitionist who volunteered in contraband camps during the war. Truth also gathered clothing, food, and supplies for African-American regiments. When the war ended, she worked to secure land for African Americans.

- Harriet Tubman, a former slave, helped dozens of enslaved blacks escape to freedom as part of the Underground Railroad and also in conjunction with the Union army.

- Hundreds of women disguised themselves as men and joined the Confederate or Union army. A few of these women wrote memoirs about their harrowing battlefield experiences, including Sarah Emma Edmonds (Union) and Loreta Janeta Velazquez (Confederacy).

KEY STATISTICS

- Women in the North and West organized approximately 7,000 women's aid societies, which were dedicated to gathering supplies and raising money for the troops. Women in the South formed more than 1,000 aid societies.

- Between 400 and 750 women disguised themselves as men and enlisted in the Union and Confederate armies.

- Approximately 300,000 women joined the workforce during the Civil War.

IMPACT ON WAR

Women played many important roles during the war, including serving as soldiers, nurses, and spies. Very early in the war, women saw an immediate need for a more efficient system for getting food, supplies, and clothing to Union soldiers. Clara Barton organized shipments to soldiers in the field. Women throughout the North and the South banded together into women's aid societies to knit, sew, and cook for the troops. Dorothea Dix worked with Henry Whitney Bellows to form the US Sanitary Commission in the North, which helped promote cleanliness and organization in field hospitals. All of these efforts helped save lives while also lifting troop morale.

IMPACT ON SOCIETY

As a result of the organizational and management skills they acquired while volunteering for social justice causes during the Civil War, women were able to create a firm foundation upon which to base the fight for women's rights in the decades that followed.

QUOTE

"I could only thank God that I was free and could go forward and work, and I was not obliged to stay at home and weep."

—*Sarah Emma Edmonds*

GLOSSARY

ABOLITIONIST
A person who wants to end slavery.

CHICORY
A root that is commonly dried, ground, and used as a substitute for coffee, especially in the South.

DYSENTERY
A bacterial disease that causes severe diarrhea.

GUERRILLA WARFARE
Attacks on civilians and troops by men or women who form their own, unofficial militia.

HARDTACK
A tough flatbread biscuit that became a staple among soldiers during the Civil War.

HOREHOUND
A bitter-tasting brown hard candy made from the horehound herb that is used to soothe a sore throat or cough, ease a stomachache, or counter asthma attacks.

IMPRESSMENT

A government policy that allows the army to seize food, crops, livestock, firewood, weapons, and men for use in the war.

INFLATION

An increase in the price of goods and services.

PIG IRON

Metal that is 92 percent iron ore.

PROFITEER

A person who buys up goods and supplies when items are scarce and sells them at high prices to make a profit.

SANCTION

To give official approval or permission.

TEMPERANCE

A movement in the 1800s and early 1900s to convince people to stop consuming alcoholic beverages.

ADDITIONAL RESOURCES

SELECTED BIBLIOGRAPHY

Blanton, DeAnne, and Lauren M. Cook. *They Fought Like Demons: Women Soldiers in the American Civil War*. Baton Rouge, LA: Louisiana State UP, 2002. Print.

Giesberg, Judith Ann. *Civil War Sisterhood: The US Sanitary Commission and Women's Politics in Transition*. Boston, MA: Northeastern UP, 2000. Print.

Silber, Nina. *Daughters of the Union: Northern Women Fight the Civil War*. Cambridge, MA: Harvard UP, 2005. Print.

FURTHER READINGS

Goldsmith, Bonnie Z. *Dr. Mary Edwards Walker: Civil War Surgeon and Medal of Honor Recipient*. Minneapolis, MN: Abdo Publishing, 2010. Print.

Hamen, Susan E. *Clara Barton: Civil War Hero and American Red Cross Founder*. Minneapolis, MN: Abdo Publishing, 2010. Print.

Morretta, Alison. *Harriet Beecher Stowe and the Abolitionist Movement*. New York: Cavendish Square, 2014. Print.

WEBSITES

To learn more about Essential Library of the Civil War, visit **booklinks.abdopublishing.com**. These links are routinely monitored and updated to provide the most current information available.

PLACES TO VISIT

African American Civil War Memorial & Museum
1925 Vermont Avenue Northwest
Washington, DC 20001
202-667-2667
http://www.afroamcivilwar.org
At this museum, learn more about the role of African-American nurses, soldiers, and spies in the Civil War.

Women's Museum of the Civil War
310 East Broadway Street
Bardstown, KY 40004
502-348-0291
http://civil-war-museum.org
This museum uses clothing and artifacts to show the roles women took on during the Civil War, including factory worker, nurse, plantation worker, soldier in disguise, and spy.

SOURCE NOTES

CHAPTER 1. A NATION DIVIDED

1. Jone Johnson Lewis. "A Nurse's View of Battle: Bull Run, First Manassas." *About.com*. 30 Nov. 2014. 25 Jan. 2016.

2. "Presidential Key Events: Abraham Lincoln." *Miller Center*. Rector and Visitors of the University of Virginia, 2016. Web. 25 Jan. 2016.

3. Mary A. Lawrence. *My Story of the War*. Hartford, CT: 1892. Google Book Search. Web. 25 Jan. 2016.

CHAPTER 2. ORGANIZING FOR A CAUSE

1. Judith Ann Giesberg. *Civil War Sisterhood: The US Sanitary Commission and Women's Politics in Transition*. Boston: Northeastern UP, 2000. Print. 5.

2. "Southern Aid Societies." The Atlantic Guard Soldiers' Aid Society. n.p., n.d. 25 Jan. 2016.

3. Nina Silber. *Daughters of the Union: Northern Women Fight the Civil War*. Cambridge, MA: Harvard UP, 2005. Print. 186.

4. Ibid. 225.

5. "Angelina Grimke Weld (1805–1879)." *Rights for Women: The Suffrage Movement and Its Leaders*. National Women's History Museum, 2007. Web. 25 Jan. 2016.

6. Nina Silber. *Daughters of the Union: Northern Women Fight the Civil War*. Cambridge, MA: Harvard UP, 2005. Print. 236.

7. Ibid.

8. Ibid. 235.

CHAPTER 3. FIGHTING AS SOLDIERS

1. Library of Congress and Middle Tennessee State University. "Women and the Civil War." *Middle Tennessee State University*. Middle Tennessee State University, n.d. Web. 25 Jan. 2016.

2. Sam Smith. "Female Soldiers in the Civil War." *Civil War Trust*. Civil War Trust, 2014. Web. 25 Jan. 2016.

3. "Sarah Emma Edmonds." *Civil War Trust*. Civil War Trust, 2014. Web. 25 Jan. 2016.

4. DeAnne Blanton and Lauren M. Cook. *They Fought Like Demons: Women Soldiers in the American Civil War*. Baton Rouge, LA: Louisiana State UP, 2002. Print. 98.

5. Rebecca Beatrice Brooks. "Loreta Janeta Velazquez: Spy and Soldier." *Civil War Saga*. n.p. 10 Jan. 2013. Web. 25 Jan. 2016.

CHAPTER 4. TENDING THE WOUNDED

1. Alice P. Stein. "Northern Volunteer Nurses of America's Civil War." *America's Civil War*, September 1999. "Civil War Nurses." *History Net*, History Net, 2016. Web. 25 Jan. 2016.

2. Ibid.

3. Ibid.

4. L. M. Alcott. "Hospital Sketches," *A Celebration of Women Writers*. University of Pennsylvania, n.d. Web. 25 Jan. 2016.

5. Robert Sattelmeyer. "Louisa May Alcott Goes to War: Eager to Support the North, the Budding Author Volunteered for a Fledgling Corps of Female Nurses." *Civil War Times*, April 2012. *History Net*. History Net, 2016. Web. 25 Jan. 2016.

6. "Union's Top Military Nurses Were Nuns," *Pittsburgh Post-Gazette*. 30 June 2013. Web. 25 Jan. 2016.

7. Alice P. Stein. "Northern Volunteer Nurses of America's Civil War." *America's Civil War*, September 1999. "Civil War Nurses." *History Net*, History Net, 2016. Web. 25 Jan. 2016.

8. "Founder Clara Barton." *American Red Cross*. American Red Cross, 2016. Web. 25 Jan. 2016.

9. "The Diary of a Civil War Nurse: Hospital Routine and Turmoil." *Smithsonian Institution*. Smithsonian National Museum of American History, n.d. Web. 25 Jan. 2016.

10. Pat Leonard. "Nursing the Union at Gettysburg." *New York Times*. New York Times, 7 July 2013. Web. 25 Jan. 2016.

11. Ibid.

12. Ibid.

13. Glenn W. LaFantasie. "Civil War Soldiers: Decimated by Disease." *History Net*. History Net, 2016. Web. 25 Jan. 2016.

CHAPTER 5. CONFEDERATE WOMEN'S WAR

1. "Death and the Civil War: General Article: The Civil War by the Numbers." *American Experience, PBS*. WGBH Educational Foundation, 2013. Web. 25 Jan. 2016.

2. Mary Boykin Miller. "Diary of Mary Chesnut. *Civil War Trust*. Civil War Trust, 2014. Web. 2 Dec. 2015.

3. "Selected Statistics on Slavery in the United States," *Civil War Causes*. n.p., n.d. Web. 25 Jan. 2016. http://civilwarcauses.org/stat.htm.

4. Ibid.

5. Milton Meltzer. *Slavery: A World History*. Cambridge, MA: Da Capo Press, 1993. Google Book Search. 25 Jan. 2016.

6. "A House Divided: 33b. Strengths and Weaknesses: North vs. South." *US History*. USHistory.org, 2014. Web. 25 Jan. 2016.

7. Tim McMahon. "Confederate Inflation Rates (1861–1865)." *InflationData.com*. Capital Professional Services, LLC, 2016. Web. 25 Jan. 2016.

8. Andrew F. Smith. *Starving the South: How the North Won the Civil War*. New York: St. Martin's Press, 2011. Print. 53.

9. "Southern Women in the Civil War." *National Humanities Center*. n.p., n.d. Web. 25 Jan. 2016.

10. Paul Escott. "Poverty and Poor Relief during the Civil War." *Encyclopedia of Virginia*. Virginia Foundation for the Humanities, 27 Oct. 2015. Web. 25. Jan. 2016.

11. Sarah Morgan Dawson. *A Confederate Girl's Diary*. New York: Houghton Mifflin, 1913. Print. 318.

12. Ibid. 317.

SOURCE NOTES
CONTINUED

CHAPTER 6. WOMEN IN THE NORTH

1. Stephen Railton. "Uncle Tom's Serialization: The *National Era* Text." *Uncle Tom's Cabin and American Culture.* University of Virginia, 2012. Web. 25 Jan. 2016.

2. "Harriet Beecher Stowe Biography." *Bio.* A&E Television Networks, 2016. Web. 25 Jan. 2016.

3. Nina Silber. *Daughters of the Union: Northern Women Fight the Civil War.* Cambridge, MA: Harvard UP, 2005. Print. 227.

4. "The War Behind the Lines: 34c. The Northern Homefront." *US History.* USHistory.org, 2014. Web. 25 Jan. 2016.

5. "Shiloh." *National Park Service.* National Park Service, Department of the Interior, and Shiloh National Military Park, Tennessee-Mississippi, n.d. 25 Jan. 2016.

6. "The War Behind the Lines: 34c. The Northern Homefront." *US History.* USHistory.org, 2014. Web. 25 Jan. 2016.

7. "Women in the Civil War." *History.* A&E Television Networks, 2016. Web. 25 Jan. 2016.

8. Nina Silber. *Daughters of the Union: Northern Women Fight the Civil War.* Cambridge, MA: Harvard UP, 2005. Print. 17.

9. Kristin Leahy. "Women during the Civil War." *Historical Society of Pennsylvania.* Historical Society of Pennsylvania, n.p. Web. 25. Jan. 2016.

10. Ibid.

11. *The Union Army: States and Regiments.* Madison, WI: Federal Publishing Company, 1908. 149. Google books.

12. "The War Behind the Lines: 34c. The Northern Homefront." *US History.* USHistory.org, 2014. Web. 25 Jan. 2016.

13. Nina Silber. *Daughters of the Union: Northern Women Fight the Civil War.* Cambridge, MA: Harvard UP, 2005. Print. 2.

14. Ibid. 228.

CHAPTER 7. AFRICAN-AMERICAN WOMEN

1. "Harriet Tubman: Underground Railroad 'Conductor,' Nurse, Spy." *Civil War Trust.* Civil War Trust, 2014. Web. 25 Jan. 2016.

2. Ibid.

3. Nina Silber. *Daughters of the Union: Northern Women Fight the Civil War.* Cambridge, MA: Harvard UP, 2005. Print. 230.

4. "From Slaves to Contraband to Free People." *Boundless U.S. History.* Boundless, 21 July 2015. Web. 25 Jan. 2016.

5. Ibid.

6. Paul Harris. "How the End of Slavery Led to Starvation and Death for Millions of Black Americans." *Guardian.* Guardian News and Media Limited, 16 June 2012. Web. 25 Jan. 2016.

7. Shiloh: Corinth Contraband Camp. *National Park Service.* National Park Service, US Department of the Interior, n.d. Web. 25 Jan. 2016.

8. Maggie MacLean. "Mary Peake." *History of American Women.* History of American Women, 28 Nov. 2014. Web. 25 Jan. 2016.

9. Ibid.

10. Ronald E. Butchart. "Susie King Taylor (1848–1912)." *New Georgia Encyclopedia.* Georgia Humanities Council and University of Georgia Press, 29 July 2013. Web. 14 Nov. 2015.

CHAPTER 8. WOMEN IN MOURNING

1. Mary Brooke Briggs Brooke. "'A Sad Day of Absorbing Interest and Distress': Women's Diaries during the War." *University of Maryland Libraries.* University of Maryland Libraries Digital Collections, 2011. Web. 25 Jan. 2016.

2. DeAnne Blanton and Lauren M. Cook. *They Fought Like Demons: Women Soldiers in the American Civil War.* Baton Rouge: Louisiana State UP, 2002. Print. 169.

3. Mary Brooke Briggs Brooke. "'A Sad Day of Absorbing Interest and Distress': Women's Diaries during the War." *University of Maryland Libraries.* University of Maryland Libraries Digital Collections, 2011. Web. 25 Jan. 2016.

4. "Death and the Civil War: Then & Now: Caring for the War's Dead and Wounded." *American Experience, PBS.* WGBH Educational Foundation, 2013. Web. 25 Jan. 2016.

5. Ibid.

6. Drew Gilpin Faust. "Death and Dying." *NPS.gov.* National Park Service, US Department of the Interior, n.d. Web. 25 Jan. 2016.

7. Ibid.

8. "Civil War Casualties: The Cost of the War: Killed, Wounded, Captured, and Missing." *Civil War Trust.* Civil War Trust, 2014. Web. 25 Jan. 2016.

9. Claire Prechtel-Kluskens. "'A Reasonable Degree of Promptitude': Civil War Pension Application Processing, 1861–1885." *Prologue,* 42.1 (2010): n. page. Web. 25 Jan. 2016.

10. Nina Silber. *Daughters of the Union: Northern Women Fight the Civil War.* Cambridge, MA: Harvard UP, 2005. Print. 269.

11. Ibid. 272.

12. "Angelina Grimke Weld (1805–1879)." *Rights for Women: The Suffrage Movement and Its Leaders.* National Women's History Museum, 2007. Web. 25 Jan. 2016.

INDEX

ABOUT THE AUTHOR

Kari Cornell is a writer and editor who loves to read, garden, cook, run, and make clever things out of nothing. She is the author of *The Nitty Gritty Gardening Book: Fun Projects for All Seasons*, *African Americans in the Civil War*, *Women on the US Homefront*, and many biographies and cookbooks for kids. She lives in Minneapolis, Minnesota, with her husband, Brian, two sons, Will and Theo, and her crazy dog, Emmylou.

ABOUT THE CONSULTANT

Bonnie Laughlin-Schultz, PhD, is a historian of the nineteenth-century United States and specializes in American women's history and the broad Civil War era. Cornell University Press published her book, *The Tie That Bound Us: The Women of John Brown's Family and the Legacy of Radical Abolitionism*, in 2013. She's currently working on a project about nineteenth-century women's rights reformers and their ideas about and experiences of motherhood, personhood, citizenship, and women's rights.